Presented to

_____

On the occasion of

_____

From

_____

Date

_____

Published by Barbour Publishing, Inc., P.O. Box 719, Uhrichsville, Ohio 44683
http://www.barbourbooks.com

Member of the
Evangelical Christian
Publishers Association

Printed in China.

A Mother's Favorite Bible Verses

BARBOUR
PUBLISHING, INC.

The eternal God
is thy refuge,
and underneath are
the everlasting arms.

DEUTERONOMY 33:27

Introduction

For generations, mothers have found comfort and encouragement in God's Word. Amidst all the challenges of childrearing, the Bible has stood as a pillar of wisdom, strength, and truth for countless mothers throughout the ages.

Collected here are many of a mother's favorite Bible verses—promises of God for provision, direction, love, and joy. Verses that offer insight into human relationships. Verses that assure mothers that God cares greatly about them—and their children. These are the Scriptures that meet mothers' deepest needs—*A Mother's Favorite Bible Verses*.

Adversity

Thou art my hiding place; thou shalt preserve me from trouble; thou shalt compass me about with songs of deliverance. Selah. PSALM 32:7

The LORD is good, a strong hold in the day of trouble; and he knoweth them that trust in him. NAHUM 1:7

These things I have spoken unto you, that in me ye might have peace. In the world ye shall have tribulation: but be of good cheer; I have overcome the world. JOHN 16:33

Beloved, think it not strange concerning the fiery trial which is to try you, as though some strange thing happened unto you:

But rejoice, inasmuch as ye are partakers of Christ's sufferings; that, when his glory shall be revealed, ye may be glad also with exceeding joy. 1 PETER 4:12–13

Blessings of Parenthood

And God Almighty bless thee, and make thee fruitful, and multiply thee, that thou mayest be a multitude of people. GENESIS 28:3

And [Esau] lifted up his eyes, and saw the women and the children; and said, Who are those with thee? And [Jacob] said, The children which God hath graciously given thy servant. GENESIS 33:5

Even by the God of thy father, who shall help thee; and by the Almighty, who shall bless thee with blessings of heaven above, blessings of the deep that lieth under, blessings of the breasts, and of the womb. . . GENESIS 49:25

He maketh the barren woman to keep house, and to be a joyful mother of children. Praise ye the LORD. PSALM 113:9

Comfort

Yea, though I walk through the valley of the shadow of death, I will fear no evil: for thou art with me; thy rod and thy staff they comfort me.   PSALM 23:4

He healeth the broken in heart, and bindeth up their wounds.   PSALM 147:3

He will swallow up death in victory; and the Lord GOD will wipe away tears from off all faces; and the rebuke of his people shall he take away from off all the earth: for the LORD hath spoken it.   ISAIAH 25:8

And I will pray the Father, and he shall give you another Comforter, that he may abide with you for ever.   JOHN 14:16

Casting all your care upon him; for he careth for you.   1 PETER 5:7

Courage

Only be thou strong and very courageous, that thou mayest observe to do according to all the law, which Moses my servant commanded thee: turn not from it to the right hand or to the left, that thou mayest prosper withersoever thou goest.   JOSHUA 1:7

Be of good courage, and he shall strengthen your heart, all ye that hope in the LORD.   PSALM 31:24

In the fear of the LORD is strong confidence: and his children shall have a place of refuge.
          PROVERBS 14:26

In whom we have boldness and access with confidence by the faith of him.   EPHESIANS 3:12

So that we may boldly say, The Lord is my helper, and I will not fear what man shall do unto me.
          HEBREWS 13:6

Diligence

I call to remembrance my song in the night: I commune with mine own heart: and my spirit made diligent search.
PSALM 77:6

Keep thy heart with all diligence; for out of it are the issues of life.
PROVERBS 4:23

Labour not for the meat which perisheth, but for that meat which endureth unto everlasting life, which the Son of man shall give unto you: for him hath God the Father sealed.
JOHN 6:27

Therefore, my beloved brethren, be ye stedfast, unmoveable, always abounding in the work of the Lord, forasmuch as ye know that your labour is not in vain in the Lord.
1 CORINTHIANS 15:58

Wherefore, beloved, seeing that ye look for such things, be diligent that ye may be found of him in peace, without spot, and blameless.
2 PETER 3:14

Encouragement

He giveth power to the faint; and to them that have no
might he increaseth strength. ISAIAH 40:29

And whether we be afflicted, it is for your consolation
and salvation, which is effectual in the enduring of the
same sufferings which we also suffer: or whether we be
comforted, it is for your consolation and salvation.
2 CORINTHIANS 1:6

Bear ye one another's burdens, and so fulfil the law of
Christ. GALATIANS 6:2

Look not every man on his own things, but every man
also on the things of others. PHILIPPIANS 2:4

Not forsaking the assembling of ourselves together, as
the manner of some is; but exhorting one another: and
so much the more, as ye see the day approaching.
HEBREWS 10:25

Eternal Life

For God so loved the world, that he gave his only begotten Son, that whosoever believeth in him should not perish, but have everlasting life.   JOHN 3:16

But whosoever drinketh of the water that I shall give him shall never thirst; but the water that I shall give him shall be in him a well of water springing up into everlasting life.   JOHN 4:14

Fight the good fight of faith, lay hold on eternal life, whereunto thou art also called, and hast professed a good profession before many witnesses.

1 TIMOTHY 6:12

And this is the record, that God hath given to us eternal life, and this life is in his Son.

He that hath the Son hath life; and he that hath not the Son of God hath not life.   1 JOHN 5:11–12

Faith

And Jesus answering saith unto them, Have faith in God.

For verily I say unto you, That whosoever shall say unto this mountain, Be thou removed, and be thou cast into the sea; and shall not doubt in his heart, but shall believe that those things which he saith shall come to pass; he shall have whatsoever he saith.

MARK 11:22–23

That your faith should not stand in the wisdom of men, but in the power of God.   1 CORINTHIANS 2:5

For by grace are ye saved through faith; and that not of yourselves: it is the gift of God.   EPHESIANS 2:8

Now faith is the substance of things hoped for, the evidence of things not seen.

But without faith it is impossible to please him: for he that cometh to God must believe that he is, and that he is a rewarder of them that diligently seek him.

HEBREWS 11:1, 6

Fear of the Lord

Only fear the LORD, and serve him in truth with all your heart: for consider how great things he hath done for you.   1 SAMUEL 12:24

The fear of the LORD is the beginning of knowledge: but fools despise wisdom and instruction.

PROVERBS 1:7

Favour is deceitful, and beauty is vain: but a woman that feareth the LORD, she shall be praised.

PROVERBS 31:30

Let us hear the conclusion of the whole matter: Fear God, and keep his commandments: for this is the whole duty of man.   ECCLESIASTES 12:13

Saying with a loud voice, Fear God, and give glory to him; for the hour of his judgment is come: and worship him that made heaven, and earth, and the sea, and the fountains of waters.   REVELATION 14:7

Forgiveness

For thou, Lord, art good, and ready to forgive; and plenteous in mercy unto all them that call upon thee.

PSALM 86:5

The discretion of a man deferreth his anger; and it is his glory to pass over a transgression.

PROVERBS 19:11

For if ye forgive men their trespasses, your heavenly Father will also forgive you.   MATTHEW 6:14

Judge not, and ye shall not be judged: condemn not, and ye shall not be condemned: forgive, and ye shall be forgiven.   LUKE 6:37

And be ye kind one to another, tenderhearted, forgiving one another, even as God for Christ's sake hath forgiven you.   EPHESIANS 4:32

Generosity

Blessed is he that considereth the poor: the LORD will deliver him in time of trouble.   PSALM 41:1

He that hath pity upon the poor lendeth unto the LORD; and that which he hath given will he pay him again.   PROVERBS 19:17

Then shall the King say unto them on his right hand, Come, ye blessed of my Father, inherit the kingdom prepared for you from the foundation of the world:
For I was an hungred, and ye gave me meat: I was thirsty, and ye gave me drink: I was a stranger, and ye took me in:
Naked, and ye clothed me: I was sick, and ye visited me: I was in prison, and ye came unto me.
And the King shall answer and say unto them, Verily I say unto you, Inasmuch as ye have done it unto one of the least of these my brethren, ye have done it unto me.   MATTHEW 25:34–36, 40

Gentleness

But the fruit of the Spirit is love, joy, peace, longsuffering, gentleness, goodness, faith.   GALATIANS 5:22

But we were gentle among you, even as a nurse cherisheth her children:

So being affectionately desirous of you, we were willing to have imparted unto you, not the gospel of God only, but also our own souls, because ye were dear unto us.   1 THESSALONIANS 2:7–8

And the servant of the Lord must not strive; but be gentle unto all men, apt to teach, patient,

In meekness instructing those that oppose themselves.   2 TIMOTHY 2:24–25

But the wisdom that is from above is first pure, then peaceable, gentle, and easy to be intreated, full of mercy and good fruits, without partiality, and without hypocrisy.   JAMES 3:17

Godly Children

The father of the righteous shall greatly rejoice: and he that begetteth a wise child shall have joy of him.

PROVERBS 23:24

Whoso loveth wisdom rejoiceth his father.

PROVERBS 29:3

Better is a poor and a wise child than an old and foolish king, who will no more be admonished.

ECCLESIASTES 4:13

When I call to remembrance the unfeigned faith that is in thee, which dwelt first in thy grandmother Lois, and thy mother Eunice; and I am persuaded that in thee also.

2 TIMOTHY 1:5

I have no greater joy than to hear that my children walk in truth.

3 JOHN 4

God's Guidance

The steps of a good man are ordered by the LORD: and he delighteth in his way. PSALM 37:23

For this God is our God for ever and ever: he will be our guide even unto death. PSALM 48:14

In all thy ways acknowledge him, and he shall direct thy paths. PROVERBS 3:6

The righteousness of the perfect shall direct his way: but the wicked shall fall by his own wickedness.

PROVERBS 11:5

And I will bring the blind by a way that they knew not; I will lead them in paths that they have not known: I will make darkness light before them, and crooked things straight. These things will I do unto them, and not forsake them. ISAIAH 42:16

Gratitude

That I may publish with the voice of thanksgiving, and tell of all thy wondrous works.   PSALM 26:7

And they, continuing daily with one accord in the temple, and breaking bread from house to house, did eat their meat with gladness and singleness of heart,
Praising God, and having favour with all the people. And the Lord added to the church daily such as should be saved.   ACTS 2:46–47

Giving thanks always for all things unto God and the Father in the name of our Lord Jesus Christ. . .
EPHESIANS 5:20

In every thing give thanks: for this is the will of God in Christ Jesus concerning you.
1 THESSALONIANS 5:18

Hope

For thou art my hope, O Lord GOD: thou art my trust from my youth.   PSALM 71:5

Blessed is the man that trusteth in the LORD, and whose hope the LORD is.   JEREMIAH 17:7

The LORD is my portion, saith my soul; therefore will I hope in him.   LAMENTATIONS 3:24

Beloved, now are we the sons of God, and it doth not yet appear what we shall be: but we know that, when he shall appear, we shall be like him; for we shall see him as he is.

And every man that hath this hope in him purifieth himself, even as he is pure.   1 JOHN 3:2–3

Humility

The fear of the LORD is the instruction of wisdom; and before honour is humility.   PROVERBS 15:33

Blessed are the poor in spirit: for theirs is the kingdom of heaven.   MATTHEW 5:3

Whosoever therefore shall humble himself as this little child, the same is greatest in the kingdom of heaven.   MATTHEW 18:4

Humble yourselves in the sight of the Lord, and he shall lift you up.   JAMES 4:10

Humble yourselves therefore under the mighty hand of God, that he may exalt you in due time.   1 PETER 5:6

For ye shall go out with joy, and be led forth with peace: the mountains and the hills shall break forth before you into singing, and all the trees of the field shall clap their hands. ISAIAH 55:12

Yet I will rejoice in the LORD, I will joy in the God of my salvation. HABAKKUK 3:18

And ye now therefore have sorrow: but I will see you again, and your heart shall rejoice, and your joy no man taketh from you. JOHN 16:22

Rejoice in the Lord alway: and again I say, Rejoice. PHILIPPIANS 4:4

Whom having not seen, ye love; in whom, though now ye see him not, yet believing, ye rejoice with joy unspeakable and full of glory. 1 PETER 1:8

Kindness

She openeth her mouth with wisdom; and in her tongue is the law of kindness.   PROVERBS 31:26

But love ye your enemies, and do good, and lend, hoping for nothing again; and your reward shall be great, and ye shall be the children of the Highest: for he is kind unto the unthankful and to the evil.

LUKE 6:35

As we have therefore opportunity, let us do good unto all men, especially unto them who are of the household of faith.   GALATIANS 6:10

Put on therefore, as the elect of God, holy and beloved, bowels of mercies, kindness, humbleness of mind, meekness, longsuffering.   COLOSSIANS 3:12

Not rendering evil for evil, or railing for railing: but contrariwise blessing; knowing that ye are thereunto called, that ye should inherit a blessing.   1 PETER 3:9

Love of God

The LORD hath appeared of old unto me, saying, Yea, I have loved thee with an everlasting love: therefore with lovingkindness have I drawn thee.

JEREMIAH 31:3

For I am persuaded, that neither death, nor life, nor angels, nor principalities, nor powers, nor things present, nor things to come,

Nor height, nor depth, nor any other creature, shall be able to separate us from the love of God, which is in Christ Jesus our Lord.   ROMANS 8:38–39

Behold, what manner of love the Father hath bestowed upon us, that we should be called the sons of God: therefore the world knoweth us not, because it knew him not.   1 JOHN 3:1

Herein is love, not that we loved God, but that he loved us, and sent his Son to be the propitiation for our sins.   1 JOHN 4:10

Love Toward Others

Be kindly affectioned one to another with brotherly love; in honour preferring one another.

ROMANS 12:10

For all the law is fulfilled in one word, even in this; Thou shalt love thy neighbour as thyself.

GALATIANS 5:14

And now abideth faith, hope, charity, these three; but the greatest of these is charity.   1 CORINTHIANS 13:13

For God hath not given us the spirit of fear; but of power, and of love, and of a sound mind.

2 TIMOTHY 1:7

Beloved, let us love one another: for love is of God; and every one that loveth is born of God, and knoweth God.

1 JOHN 4:7

Meekness

The meek shall eat and be satisfied: they shall praise the LORD that seek him: your heart shall live for ever.

PSALM 22:26

For the LORD taketh pleasure in his people: he will beautify the meek with salvation.   PSALM 149:4

The meek also shall increase their joy in the LORD, and the poor among men shall rejoice in the Holy One of Israel.   ISAIAH 29:19

Seek ye the LORD, all ye meek of the earth, which have wrought his judgment; seek righteousness, seek meekness: it may be ye shall be hid in the day of the LORD 's anger.   ZEPHANIAH 2:3

Blessed are the meek: for they shall inherit the earth.

MATTHEW 5:5

Mercy

The LORD is good to all: and his tender mercies are over all his works.
PSALM 145:9

Let not mercy and truth forsake thee: bind them about thy neck; write them upon the table of thine heart:
So shalt thou find favour and good understanding in the sight of God and man.
PROVERBS 3:3–4

Therefore turn thou to thy God: keep mercy and judgment and wait on thy God continually.
HOSEA 12:6

Blessed are the merciful: for they shall obtain mercy.
MATTHEW 5:7

Behold, we count them happy which endure. Ye have heard of the patience of Job, and have seen the end of the Lord; that the Lord is very pitiful, and of tender mercy.
JAMES 5:11

Our Good Shepherd

The LORD is my shepherd; I shall not want.

PSALM 23:1

He shall feed his flock like a shepherd: he shall gather the lambs with his arm, and carry them in his bosom, and shall gently lead those that are with young.

ISAIAH 40:11

I am the good shepherd: the good shepherd giveth his life for the sheep.

I am the good shepherd, and know my sheep, and am known of mine.

JOHN 10:11, 14

For the Lamb which is in the midst of the throne shall feed them, and shall lead them unto living fountains of waters: and God shall wipe away all tears from their eyes.

REVELATION 7:17

Patience

In your patience possess ye your souls.   LUKE 21:19

And let us not be weary in well doing: for in due season we shall reap, if we faint not.   GALATIANS 6:9

And the servant of the Lord must not strive; but be gentle unto all men, apt to teach, patient.

2 TIMOTHY 2:24

For ye have need of patience, that, after ye have done the will of God, ye might receive the promise.

HEBREWS 10:36

Knowing this, that the trying of your faith worketh patience.

But let patience have her perfect work, that ye may be perfect and entire, wanting nothing.   JAMES 1:3–4

The LORD will give strength unto his people; the LORD will bless his people with peace.   PSALM 29:11

Thou wilt keep him in perfect peace, whose mind is stayed on thee: because he trusteth in thee.
                                                                    ISAIAH 26:3

Now the God of hope fill you with all joy and peace in believing, that ye may abound in hope, through the power of the Holy Ghost.   ROMANS 15:13

And the peace of God, which passeth all understanding, shall keep your hearts and minds through Christ Jesus.   PHILIPPIANS 4:7

And the fruit of righteousness is sown in peace of them that make peace.   JAMES 3:18

Prayer

Thou shalt make thy prayer unto him, and he shall hear thee, and thou shalt pay thy vows.   JOB 22:27

Ask, and it shall be given you; seek, and ye shall find; knock, and it shall be opened unto you:
     For every one that asketh receiveth; and he that seeketh findeth; and to him that knocketh it shall be opened.   MATTHEW 7:7–8

Pray without ceasing.   1 THESSALONIANS 5:17

Let us therefore come boldly unto the throne of grace, that we may obtain mercy, and find grace to help in time of need.   HEBREWS 4:16

The effectual fervent prayer of a righteous man availeth much.   JAMES 5:16

Protection

Be thou my strong habitation, whereunto I may continually resort: thou hast given commandment to save me; for thou art my rock and my fortress.   PSALM 71:3

The name of the LORD is a strong tower: the righteous runneth into it, and is safe.   PROVERBS 18:10

When thou passest through the waters, I will be with thee; and through the rivers, they shall not overflow thee: when thou walkest through the fire, thou shalt not be burned; neither shall the flame kindle upon thee.   ISAIAH 43:2

Who is like unto thee, O people saved by the LORD, the shield of they help, and who is the sword of thy excellency!   DEUTERONOMY 33:29

Above all, taking the shield of faith, wherewith ye shall be able to quench all the fiery darts of the wicked.   EPHESIANS 6:16

Repentance

The LORD is nigh unto them that are of a broken heart; and saveth such as be of a contrite spirit.

PSALM 34:18

He that covereth his sins shall not prosper: but whoso confesseth and forsaketh them shall have mercy.

PROVERBS 28:13

And saying, The time is fulfilled, and the kingdom of God is at hand: repent ye, and believe the gospel.

MARK 1:15

Likewise, I say unto you, there is joy in the presence of the angels of God over one sinner that repenteth.

LUKE 15:10

The Lord is not slack concerning his promise, as some men count slackness; but is longsuffering to us-ward, not willing that any should perish, but that all should come to repentance.

2 PETER 3:9

Rest

And thou shalt be secure, because there is hope; yea, thou shalt dig about thee, and thou shalt take thy rest in safety.   JOB 11:18

I will both lay me down in peace, and sleep: for thou, LORD, only makest me dwell in safety.   PSALM 4:8

When thou liest down, thou shalt not be afraid: yea, thou shalt lie down, and thy sleep shall be sweet.
                                        PROVERBS 3:24

Come unto me, all ye that labour and are heavy laden, and I will give you rest.
    Take my yoke upon you, and learn of me; for I am meek and lowly in heart: and ye shall find rest unto your souls.   MATTHEW 11:28–29

Salvation

Jesus answered, Verily, verily, I say unto thee, Except a man be born of water and of the Spirit, he cannot enter into the kingdom of God.

That which is born of the flesh is flesh; and that which is born of the Spirit is spirit.

Marvel not that I said unto thee, Ye must be born again.
JOHN 3:5–7

For he hath made him to be sin for us, who knew no sin; that we might be made the righteousness of God in him.
2 CORINTHIANS 5:21

In whom we have redemption through his blood, the forgiveness of sins, according to the riches of his grace. . .
EPHESIANS 1:7

For this is good and acceptable in the sight of God our Saviour;

Who will have all men to be saved, and to come unto the knowledge of the truth.
1 TIMOTHY 2:3–4

Temptation

And lead us not into temptation, but deliver us from evil: For thine is the kingdom, and the power, and the glory, for ever. Amen.   MATTHEW 6:13

There hath no temptation taken you but such as is common to man: but God is faithful, who will not suffer you to be tempted above that ye are able; but will with the temptation also make a way to escape, that ye may be able to bear it.   1 CORINTHIANS 10:13

Blessed is the man that endureth temptation: for when he is tried, he shall receive the crown of life, which the Lord hath promised to them that love him.
                                                    JAMES 1:12

The Lord knoweth how to deliver the godly out of temptations, and to reserve the unjust unto the day of judgment to be punished.   2 PETER 2:9

Training Children

And if it seem evil unto you to serve the LORD, choose you this day whom ye will serve; whether the gods which your fathers served that were on the other side of the flood, or the gods of the Amorites, in whose land ye dwell: but as for me and my house, we will serve the LORD.   JOSHUA 24:15

Come, ye children, hearken unto me: I will teach you the fear of the LORD.   PSALM 34:11

Chasten thy son while there is hope, and let not thy soul spare for his crying.   PROVERBS 19:18

Train up a child in the way he should go: and when he is old, he will not depart from it.   PROVERBS 22:6

Correct thy son, and he shall give thee rest; yea, he shall give delight unto thy soul.   PROVERBS 29:17

Trust in God

The God of my rock; in him will I trust: he is my shield, and the horn of my salvation, my high tower, and my refuge, my saviour; thou savest me from violence.

2 SAMUEL 22:3

Blessed is that man that maketh the LORD his trust, and respecteth not the proud, nor such as turn aside to lies.

PSALM 40:4

I will say of the LORD, He is my refuge and my fortress: my God; in him will I trust.

PSALM 91:2

Trust in the LORD with all thine heart; and lean not unto thine own understanding.

PROVERBS 3:5

And such trust have we through Christ to God-ward.

2 CORINTHIANS 3:4

Wisdom

Say unto wisdom, Thou art my sister; and call under-standing thy kinswoman.   PROVERBS 7:4

For God giveth to a man that is good in his sight wis-dom, and knowledge, and joy.   ECCLESIASTES 2:26

Therefore whosoever heareth these sayings of mine, and doeth them, I will liken him unto a wise man, which built his house upon a rock:
    And the rain descended, and the floods came, and the winds blew, and beat upon that house; and it fell not: for it was founded upon a rock.
                                              MATTHEW 7:24–25

If any of you lack wisdom, let him ask of God, that giveth to all men liberally, and upbraideth not; and it shall be given him.   JAMES 1:5